SIMPLIFIED FINANCIAL MANAGEMENT

A SELF EXPLANATORY APPROACH

BY

MXOLISI NDLOVU

SIMPLIFIED FINANCIAL MANAGEMENT

Copyright © Mxolisi Ndlovu, 2017

ISBN: 978-1-7187-5583-3

Contact details

Email: mxolisi.mxndlovu@gmail.com

Skype: mxolisi.ndlovu1

Cell: +263773515645

All rights reserved. This book is protected under International Copyright Law. It may not be copied or reprinted for commercial gain or profit. The use of short quotations or occasional page copying for personal or group study is permitted and encouraged. Permission will be granted upon request.

Cover Design and Interior Page Layout by **Pearl Press Media**
Printed and Published by Pearl Press Media
www.pearlpressmedia.co.zw
Email: pearlpressmedia@gmail.com

TABLE OF CONTENTS

ABOUT THE AUTHOR 5
ACKNOWLEDGEMENTS 6
INTRODUCTION TO FINANCIAL MANAGEMENT 7
What is financial management? 7
The role of the financial manager 7
Goals of financial management 8
FINANCIAL SYSTEM 9
Financial & Capital Markets 9
Functions of financial system 10
Time value of money 10
Theories that explain the structure of interest rates 11
FINANCIAL PLANNING 13
Capital Budgeting 13
Cost of Capital 17
WORKING CAPITAL MANAGEMENT 21
Working Capital policies 22
Receivables management 22
Credit Standards 22
Control 24
CASH MANAGEMENT 25
Cash Operating Cycle **25**
Banking policy 26
Cash management models 27
Inventory Management 28
SOURCES OF CAPITAL 30
Financial Markets 30
Types of Capital 30
Capitalization 33
Capital Structure **34**

PROFIT MANAGEMENT 37
Dividend Policy 37
Dividend Policy Theories 38
FINANCIAL RATIOS 41
Classification OF Ratios 41
Liquidity Ratios 43
Profitability and Activity ratios 43
FUNDS FLOW AND CASHFLOW STATEMENTS 45
Cash flow Statements 45
Funds Flow Statements 46
BUDGETS AND BUDGETORY CONTROL SYSTEMS 47
CORPORATE RESTRUCTURING 50
INTERNATIONAL BUSINESS FINANCE 53
Forms of risk arising from international operations 54
The Foreign Exchange Market 54
CREDIT RATING 56
ASSETS AND LIABILITIES MANAGEMENT 58
Gap Analysis 59
BIBLIOGRAPHY 61

ABOUT THE AUTHOR

Mxolisi Ndlovu was born in 1978 at Umzingwane district in Matabeleland South. He did his Primary education at Kumbudzi Primary School and His secondary education at Bezha Secondary in Umzingwane.

He then went on to do Institute of Certified Bookkeepers Certificate before enrolling at Bulawayo Polytechnic where he did Certificate in Business Studies and National Diploma in Accountancy as well as Cert in Business Function from Zimbabwe Institute of Management. He then enrolled with the Zimbabwe Open University where he completed His Bachelors of Commerce in Accounting Degree. Mr Ndlovu also holds an MBA-Finance degree from Assam Don Bosco University India.

Mr Mxolisi Ndlovu has vast experience in the Field of Accounting and Finance having worked in Business Consultancy, Light Steel, manufacturing and Hospitality Industries for almost 20 years. He currently works as an Accountant for one of the top Hotel Chains in Zimbabwe and also serving as the National Treasurer of Zimbabwe Volleyball Association.

He is a renowned sports administrator who has served in the Bulawayo Sports Board and has been serving the Zimbabwe Volleyball Association Board since 2008 to date. He also holds Certificates in Sports Administration, Volleyball information system and Sports Nutrition.

Mr Ndlovu is a family man, married with three daughters.

ACKNOWLEDGEMENTS

I want to thank my family for being on my side as I was putting together this piece of work.

INTRODUCTION TO FINANCIAL MANAGEMENT

What is financial management?

This deals with financial analysis, planning and control, acquisition and effective employment of funds in order to maximise the value of the firm; and as well as to achieve its business objectives.

Fundamentals of financial management

The relevant objectives in financial management are the maximising of certain variables such as;

a) Profit
b) Share price
c) Investor's wealth or growth

The important thing is to establish which variable should be maximised at the expense of the others.

Financial management focuses on principles of decision making. Decision making is the selection of one course of action from two or more alternative courses of action. These decisions require that appropriate estimations be made. The variables on which financial management focuses as the primary input in decision making are: EXPECTED RETURN AND PERCIEVED RISK.

The role of the financial manager

A financial manager is responsible for the financial health of an organization. As a result, the manager's role is:

1. To pursue wealth creating investment opportunities.
2. To look for funds to finance the investment.

Investment decisions

This is concerned with how the firm allocates its resources to assets that generate income at the present moment as well as in future. These include capital budgeting processes and techniques, capital rationing, financial markets and security price analysis.

Financing decisions

These are concerned with raising of funds to finance corporate assets. The decisions include considering the sources and forms of finance, capital structure, cost of capital and dividend decisions.

Goals of financial management

As we have defined what financial management is, the goals of financial management are therefore laid out thus:

- Profit maximization
- Sales maximization
- Costs minimization
- Survival of the firm
- Capturing of market share
- Being a market leader
- Maximizing remuneration to executive
- Minimizing staff turnover.

FINANCIAL SYSTEM

Financial & Capital Markets

Financial system includes both financial markets and capital markets.

Financial markets — These include the foreign exchange, fixed-income and equity markets, as well as the new and growing markets for derivatives securities such as futures, options and swaps.

Capital markets — The function of capital market is also performed by financial intermediaries such as banks and insurance companies, which provide customized products and services- the kind that do not lend themselves to the standardization necessary to support a liquid market.

Capital markets includes the following securities –

1. Equity – These are shares of public listed companies which are traded on the stock exchange. The investor in equity market expects a return in the form of a divided.

    ### Types of shares

    a. Ordinary shares – These types of shares are entitled to their dividends if they are declared on the residual income. If the dividends are not declared on that year, the investor will not accrue any dividend for the year.
    b. Preference shares – These are shares which earn fixed rate preference dividends and they accrue their respective dividend whether there are profits or not.

2. Debt – This is usually in the form of bonds which are issued by companies in order to borrow from the public so as to raise capital. Bonds usually last for a fixed period of time and earn a fixed interest rate.

Functions of financial system

- To provide ways of clearing and settling payments to facilitate trade.
- To provide a mechanism for the pooling of resources and for the subdividing of shares in various enterprises.
- To provide ways to transfer economic resources through time, across borders, and among industries.
- To provide ways of managing risk.
- To provide price information to help coordinate decentralized decision-making in various sectors of the economy.
- To provide ways of dealing with the incentive problems created when one party to a transaction has information that the other party does not or when party acts as agent for the other.

Time value of money

People generally prefer to receive money sooner rather than later. Money can be used to earn more money and that is why people prefer to receive money sooner than later. The principle is that the earlier cash is received the greater the potential for increasing wealth. Therefore compensation is required for someone to forego the use of money for some specified time.

When someone is loaned some money there is uncertainty that the money will be repaid. This risk of capital not being repaid means the one who is borrowing money has to pay a cost for that. This premium should be in line with the risk taken.

Inflation

In times of rising prices it is clear that the purchasing power of money decreases overtime. Any lender would expect compensation for the decline in the spending power of that money overtime. That compensation is called interest and a certain rate of interest is charged on the money loaned.

Interest rates can be expressed as the function of the following variables.

1. The time value of money
2. Inflation
3. Risk of the capital not being repaid

Theories that explain the structure of interest rates

The expectations theory

Every investor would clearly hope at the end of a year to be at least as wealthy as the result of an investment as at the beginning of the year. The interest received should therefore at least compensate for the loss of the purchasing power due to inflation. In short the theory holds that on the yield curve the slope of the term structure of interest rates depends on the expected future spot rates of the interest.

The liquidity preference theory

This theory tries to introduce the element of risk as it explains the structure of interest rates. The risk is not related to default on capital invested, but rather to interest rate fluctuations. For example; if you hold both a twenty year and a one year investment, each with a coupon rate of 12%, when the market rate of interest is 12%. If expected inflation increases the market rate, the negative effect on the value of a 20 year investment would be far greater than on the 1 year investment. Therefore the interest rate risk is greater when the period to maturity of an investment is longer.

Future and present values

Future value is the value in dollar terms at some point in future of an investment or a series of investments (Carlos Correia, Financial Management, 2nd impression 1995). It can also be defined as the amount of cash which will have accrued by a given date resulting from earlier lump-sum or periodic investments.

This can be calculated using the formulae $FV = PV(1+r)$ for one period and $FV = PV(1+r)^n$ for more than one period where:

FV is the amount accrued by a given date as a result from earlier lump sum or periodic investments.

PV is the value of investment at the beginning of the period or the principal amount.

r is the rate of interest

n is the number of periods to which the investment is to receive interest.

Present value is defined by Carlos Correia as the value today, of a stream of expected future cash flows. The present value can be calculated by discounting future cash flows.

The formulae for calculating Present Value is as follows:

$PV = FV(1+r)^n$

FINANCIAL PLANNING

Financial planning is the establishment of standards such as budgets so that we can make financial comparisons with the actual performance. A budget will organize a firm's finances and at times includes a chain of specific goals for spending and saving in the future. This plan is sometimes called an investment plan.

The preparation of these budgets is a planning function while the administering is the controlling function; according to Sukkim and Seng H. Kim, Global corporate finance, 6th edition, 2006

This involves the process of budget preparation, profit planning and analysis of corporate gearing.

All these skills are critical in financial management as they are used in corporate finance decision such as cash management, capital budgeting, capital structure and security investment analysis.

Purpose of Planning

-To provide a clear detailed direction of the firm which results in less uncertainty and proper direction.

-To set out expectations of the firm for that concerned period.

-To provide means of measuring and controlling performance for that period.

-Achieving greater coordination of different activities of the firm.

Capital Budgeting

This is the evaluation and analysis of investment projects which normally produce benefits over a number of years. In other words, capital budgeting or investment appraisal involves the planning process used to decide whether an organization's long term investments projects are worth the funding of cash. This may result in a firm tying up funds for a number of years.

TYPES OF INVESTMENT PROJECTS

Replacement or expansion

Replacement refers to the acquisition of an asset to maintain existing production. The new investment may result in savings due to increased efficiencies.

Capital budget terminology

Independent project- This is where one project does not affect, or is not affected by the acceptance of another project.

Mutually exclusive projects- These are projects which cannot be undertaken at the same time.

Divisible project- This is a project which can be split into smaller parts capable of being undertaken separately.

Indivisible project- This is a project which cannot be split into smaller parts. Such a project has to be accepted or rejected as a whole.

In capital budgeting only incremental cash flows and opportunity costs and benefits are relevant for decision –making purposes. These relate to actual or imputed inflows and outflows which occur only if the project is undertaken. Overhead costs should only be allocated to a project if they are directly related to it. Depreciation is not included in the cash flow estimates for capital investment decision as it is a non-cash expense.

CAPITAL BUDGETING METHODS

Methods used for capital budgeting are;

1. Net present value
2. Internal rate of return
3. Payback method
4. Accounting rate of return

Net present value (NPV)

This method takes into account the time value of money. It is used in Capital Budgeting to analyse the profitability of a project. According to Carlos Correia it involves estimating a project's future cash flows, discounting these cash flows at company's required rate of return (cost of capital), and subtracting cost of investment from the present value. If the result is positive, it means that the project results in an increase in shareholders' wealth as the project earns more than earns the required rate of return. In general, a project with a positive NPV will be a profitable one.

Example

Project B has the following cash flow stream

Year 0   -$10000.00

Year 1 $8000.00

Year 2 $6000.00

The cost of capital is 20%

	Cash flow	PV Factor	Present value
Cost	-10000.00	1.00	-10000.00
Year 1	8000.00	0.833	6664.00
Year 2	6000.00	0.694	4164.00
NET PRESENT VALUE			**828.00**

The project B has a positive NPV, and should therefore be accepted. This means that the shareholders' wealth will be increased.

Internal rate of return (IRR)

The IRR is the discount rate which causes the present value of net future cash flows to equal the cost of the investment.

Usually you will need to calculate the internal rate of return which will produce zero NPV; therefore you will have to go do through trial and error method.

After doing that you will then have to compare the IRR with the cost of capital. If the project's IRR is greater than the cost of capital, then the project should be accepted as it offers a higher return than the cost of financing it the project.

Payback period

This measures the time it takes for the firm to recover the cost of the investment from cash flows generated by the project. This mainly indicates the length of the period how long the funds will be at risk. Where the projects earns equal cash flows every year the formulae for calculating the payback period is:

$$\frac{\text{Cost of investment}}{\text{Annual cash flow}}$$

The payback period method has a disadvantage that it ignores the cash flows after the payback period; therefore it is not a profitability indicator and creates a bias against long-term projects.

It ignores time value for money as it assumes that the time value of money is zero.

ACCOUNTING RATE OF RETURN

The return on investment is used to measure the effectiveness with which management is utilizing the assets of the company. Management is often evaluated according to this ratio, which is based on the book value of the assets. The Accounting Rate of Return (ARR) formula is as follows:

ARR= average incremental net income / average investment

Average incremental net income is the expected annual average increase in net income if the project is accepted. This is ascertained by dividing total net income of the project by its economic useful life.

Net income is income after deducting depreciation and other non cash items.

RISK AND RETURN IN CAPITAL BUDGETING

The evaluation of project risk is based on probability distributions and expected values. This is according to Carlos Corriea.

Expected value and probability distributions

Risk is measured by the variability of a project's future cash flows. Therefore we need to calculate the expected value.

To quantify risk we need a measurement of the variability of cash flows around this expected value. The standard deviation measures the spread of possible cash flows around the mean or expected value. In comparing investment projects, we can compare standard deviations to determine relative levels of risk. The standard deviations of various projects are, however, not directly comparable if the projects have different expected values. The coefficient of variation expresses the standard deviation per unit of expected value, that is, it measurers the risk relative to return. This is computed as follows: project standard deviation/expected value

A project with a low coefficient of variation will reflect low risk.

Example

Project	STD deviation	expected return	coefficient of variation
A	15000.00	32000.00	0.47
B	5000.00	25000.00	0.20

Project A has a high expected return, but high coefficient of variation. Therefore the project is of high risk than project B.

Cost of Capital

Firms incur financing costs, when they raise funds for financing their project. The cost of capital is the rate that is used to discount the project cash flows.

a. If a company is funded by 100% equity, its cost of capital is the cost of equity.
b. If a company is funded by debt, its cost of capital is the cost of debt.
c. If a company is funded by preferred stock the cost of capital is the cost of preferred stock.
d. If a company is funded by debt equity and preferred stock the pool of funds theory requires that each individual source of capital loses to the pool of funds cost of capital and a cost would be the weighted average of all the sources.

Cost of equity

The cost of equity is the rate expected by shareholders.

For a low growth dividend: $P_O = D_O/K_e$

This means that $K_e = D_O/P_O$

Where K_e = cost of equity

D_o = dividend

P_O = Value of stock

Constant growth model

Dividends do not usually remain constant as is typical for dividends to grow.

Therefore $P_O = D_1/K_e - g$

This is = $K_e = D_1/P_O + g$

Example

A firm that has just paid a dividend of 20cents per share and its shares are currently selling at $2.00 each. The dividends are expected to grow at a rate of 10% per annum for ever. Calculate the cost of equity.

$K_e = 0.2/2 + 0.1 = 0.2$

The cost of capital is 20%

Cost of new shares

When a firm raises new funds it incurs substantial stocks in the form of floatation costs charged by investments banking firms for their services for assisting in the selling of shares. Such cost usually reduce the amount received by firms. Therefore the formula for calculating cost of new shares is as follows: $K_e = D_1/P_O (1-f) + g$

f = floatation costs per unit

Cost of debt

This refers to interest-bearing loans. These loans are at a negotiated rate and registered debentures at a coupon rate.

The formula for calculating cost of debt is $K_d = I(1-t)$

Where K_d = the cost of debt

    I = the interest rate payable

    t = the marginal tax rate

Interest is a tax deductible expense. Therefore a company serves on its taxable income by deducting the interest, therefore the effective cost of debt must be the after tax cost of the debt.

Measuring the overall cost of capital

Weighted average cost of capital (WACC)

In determining the weighted average cost of capital the premise is that the total amount of capital remains constant although the capital structure may change.

To compute a firm's WACC requires the following:

1. Compute the cost of capital for each source of financing debt, preferred and common stock
2. Determine the percentage of debt, preferred and common stock to be used in the financing of future investments.
3. Calculate the firm's WACC using the percentage of financing as the weights.

WACC is found by weighting the cost of each individual component of capital by its proportion in the firm's capital structure.

The weights to be used could be book values or market values

$WACC = K_d(1-T)w_d + K_P(w_p) + K_S W_S$

EXAMPLE

SOURCE	COST	WEIGHT	CONTRIBUTION
EQUITY	25%	0.6	15.00
PREFFERED	21.8%	0.1	2.18

DEBT	12%	0.3	3.60
WACC			**20.78%**

Assume all of them are after tax including debt

$K_C = 25(0.6) + 21.8(0.1) + 12(0.3)$

$= 15 + 2.18 + 3.6$

$= \underline{\mathbf{20.78\%}}$

WORKING CAPITAL MANAGEMENT

Working capital is referred to as current assets which are used for the day to day running of the business. Net working capital is the total of current assets less current liabilities. Working capital management involves the administration, within policy guidelines, of current assets and liabilities.

Objectives of working capital management

Certain levels of working capital are required for the firm to operate efficiently. If the levels of stock are too low the firm will be exposed to certain risk. Low stock levels might result in stock run outs therefore resulting in loss of margins. Low levels of debtors as a result of strict collection policies might force customers to buy somewhere else. Low levels of cash result in the firm not being able to meet some commitments. On the other hand, high levels of working capital will result in money tied up in working capital and not earning a return. Therefore when determining the levels of working capital you need to balance risk and return.

The working capital cycle

The working capital cycle knowledge will help one to put up essential working capital policy.

An example of the working capital cycle in a hotel is as follows:

- The hotel will order food, drinks and room amenities required by customers.
- This transaction will either reduce cash balance or increase accounts payable.
- Labour is used to convert the food materials into main meals and room amenities are placed in rooms for use by customers.
- Prepared menus and rooms will be sold to customers. Cash sales will increase cash and credit sales will increase accounts receivables.
- Creditors will require payment which will lead into cash reduction.
- The cycle is finally completed when we receive cash from debtors and we can then repeat the cycle.

Working Capital policies

Working capital policy involves basically two decisions which are as follows:

1. The appropriate level of current assets
2. How to finance those current assets.

There is a relationship between the level of asset investment and risk. The greater the level of output the less risky the firm's working capital policy. This means risk of shortages which would disturb the production or sales and lead to increased costs or decreased sales is reduced.

If they are high levels of stock there are little chances of stock run out and production disruption. Also high cash levels will enable the firm to honour up on its cash requirements and will be able to extend credit periods to debtors, thereby preventing loss in sales as a result of stringent credit conditions.

Receivables management

Debtors constitute a major component of working capital hence they require planning and control. The debtors' management policies have an impact on the value maximization of the firm.

The credit policy requires decisions to be made on the following:

1. Credit standards
2. Credit terms
3. Collection and control

Credit Standards

Whether the firm should offer credit or not it should be influenced by the factors below:

- The level of competition.
  This therefore means that if the industry is highly competitive the firm might have to offer credit.

- Tradition of the industry.
- Competitors.

If the firm decides to offer credit it should formulate standards which will achieve the following:

- Offer credit to customers who will pay on time
- Refuse credit to customers who are likely to default.
- Grant credit to slow paying customers only when, or if, the net return is positive.

To analyse the credit worthiness of the customer we use the following:

Character   - willingness to pay

Capacity   - the ability to pay

Capital   - financial reserves or the net worth of the customer.

Collateral - pledged assets

Conditions - relevant economic conditions

In analysing the credit information of customers you use the following

1. Judgement
2. Ration analysis
3. A scoring system
4. Statistical analysis

Credit terms

Credit terms should be determined in the light of the needs of the firm and the standard credit terms of the industry.

Pricing of products must take into account the credit period offered by the firm.

Therefore Credit price = Cash + $\frac{\text{Credit Period}}{365}$ x Cost of funds x Cash price

The firm should determine the amount of discount after careful considering the effective rate of offering cash discount, which is computed as follows;

Effective rate of offering cash discount =

$$\frac{\text{Discount\%}}{100\% - \text{discount\%}} \quad x \quad \frac{365}{\text{total credit period - discount period}}$$

If the firm cannot achieve a higher rate of return than the effective rate of cash discount then the firm should not adopt the cash discount term.

Collection and Control

Collection may be done in the manner below;

- Send a reminder to the defaulting customer.
- Make use of collection agency
- Take legal action
- Declare bad debt

Credit collection policies can reduce the need for working capital in order for the business to sustain its operations. The collection policies will reduce the need for short term funding.

Control

There must be a system which will ensure that customers are complying with credit terms and also check whether there are factors which cause the customers not to comply.

These can be through the production of aged debtors report and the debtors' payment pattern report.

The following ideas can help the firm collect money from debtors;

- Develop appropriate procedures for handling late payments.
- Track and pursue late payers.
- Get external help if your own efforts fail.
- Do not feel guilty asking for money, it is yours and you are entitled to it.
- Make a call now and keep asking until you get satisfaction.
- In difficult circumstances take what you can now and agree terms for the remainder. It lessens the problem.
- When asking for money, it should be hard on the issue but soft on the person. Do not give the debtor any excuses for not paying.
- Make it your objective to get the money.

CASH MANAGEMENT

According to Carlos Corriea the firm has four main reasons to hold cash which are as follows:

1. To do transactions
2. As a precautionary measure
3. As a speculative measure
4. Loan covenants

The major objective when it comes to cash management is to make sure that cash balances are minimized as cash is not an earning asset. This will actually optimise overall fund utilization. Keeping too much cash will not give much value as cash does not necessarily earn a return.

Cash Operating Cycle

There are two elements in the business cycle that absorb cash namely: inventory and debtors.

In working capital management time is money; meaning if you manage to collect money fast from debtors you will be able to both reduce the need to borrow money as well as increase to you cash to fund the working capital. This will reduce to you interest on borrowed funds and you can have some money to take care of sales growth.

The cash operating cycle is as follows:

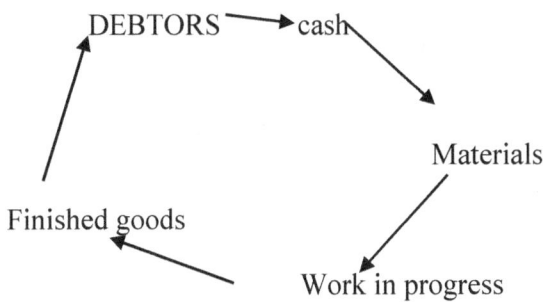

The operating cycle represents the time cash is tied up in operations of the firm from the period raw materials are acquired up to the time cash is received from debtors who had bought finished goods.

For us to calculate the cycle we need to take into consideration the conversion periods. These are as follows:

1. Raw material conversion time (RMCT) - This is the average period from the day of purchase to when they actually enter into the production system.
2. Creditor's conversion time (CCT) - This is the period from purchase of raw materials on credit to when the firm finally makes cash payment.
3. Work in progress conversion time (WIPCCT) - This is the average time it takes to convert a unit of raw materials into a finished product.
4. Finished goods conversion time (FGCCT) - This is the average time that takes to sell goods that have come from production process.
5. Debtors' conversion time (DCCT) - This is the average time that it takes to sell goods that have come through the production process.

The calculation of the cash operating cycle (COC) is as follows:

COC = RMCT- CCT + WIPCCT + FGCCT + DCCT

The creditors' conversion period is deducted when calculating the cash operating cycle as we will not have paid cash for the raw materials.

The shorter the COC the lower the opportunity cost of tying funds in business operations.

Banking policy

The firm should establish the clear banking policy which includes the following:

- Receipts and disbursements
- The criteria of selecting a bank
- Determination of the optimal banking frequency

Management of cash receipts and disbursements

Cash receipts

- You should know who opens mail, receives cheques and accepts cash payments.
- How, where and by whom they are recorded
- The actual banking procedure

Cash disbursement

- The origination of payments
- Requisition procedures must be in place
- Disbursement of cheques
- Accounting for funds
- Control on the bank account of the firm

CHOICE OF BANK

When choosing the bank you need to consider the following

1. Credit facility available
2. International structure of the bank
3. The service charge and structure
4. Consider the size of the bank in relation to that of the company
5. Issue of goodwill such as the reputation of the bank

Cash management models

The Baumol model

This model is derived from the economic order quantity model and assumes that the firm can instantly replenish its cash position and gradually use the available cash resources. This model considers the trade-off between fixed cost of raising cash by selling marketable securities and the opportunity cost of holding cash. The objective of the Baumol model is to minimize opportunity costs as well as trading costs.

The Miller Orr model

The objective of this model is to

- Determine the amount of money market securities the firm should purchase when the upper limit of cash is reached.

- Derive the amount of money market securities that should be sold when the firm reaches a lower limit of cash.

Inventory Management

Inventory management involve the management of the following:

1. Raw materials and components
2. Work in progress
3. Finished goods
4. Stores and spares

The advantages of inventory are:

- Economies of production
- Economies in procurement
- Quick delivery to customers
- Flexibility

The disadvantages of inventory are:

- Inventory investments represents opportunity forgone to invest or to reinvest funds
- The firm incurs costs of inventory management

The amount of inventory that a firm holds depends on the following factors;

1. Frequency of use
2. Sources of supply
3. Lead time
4. Physical characteristics
5. Cost

Inventory has the following cost:

- Ordering and acquisition cost
- Carrying costs
- Costs of under stocking or stock run outs

Economic order quantity (EOQ)

This is a model that is used to determine the optimal order quantity that will lead to reduced ordering and carrying costs.

The formulae for calculating EOQ is as follows:

$$EOQ = \sqrt{\frac{2 \times \text{Annual demand} \times \text{ordering cost per order}}{\text{Carrying cost per unit per year}}}$$

JUST IN TIME (JIT) PRODUCTION

This management philosophy tries to eliminate the costs of manufacturing waste by producing the right part in the right place at the right time. The philosophy focuses on the following;

- Reduction of inventory levels thereby increasing inventory turnover rate
- Improving product quality
- Reduction of delivery and production lead times
- Reducing other costs, e.g. machine set-up cost.

SOURCES OF CAPITAL

Financial Markets

This is a market place where financial assets are traded. The markets are classified as follows:

Money and capital markets

Money market is used for raising short-term finance and is usually operated by financial institutions such as commercial banks and merchant banks; as well as finance houses.

Capital market is used to trade long-term finance and is operated by the stock exchange.

Primary and secondary markets

Primary market is the market of new issues of finance. When the company goes to the market to raise funds this is the primary market.

Secondary market is where securities already issued are traded. This is the market which gives the market value of securities respectively.

Spot and derivative market

Spot market is where instruments are traded at the agreed price immediately, whereas derivative market is where settlement is deferred. The use of derivative instruments enables the creation of finance to suit the particular needs of lenders and borrowers. This is according to Carlos Corriea.

Types of Capital

EQUITY CAPITAL

This is the source of capital that is provided by the owners themselves. In the case of a corporate, it comprises of share capital and retained earnings.

Types of shares

Ordinary shares

With these shares the interest of the shareholders is directly linked to the performance of the company. The shareholders get dividends after the payment of all other dues from the profit; and the higher the returns the higher the dividends paid to ordinary shareholders.

Preference shares

These have both the characteristics of equity and debt capital. They promise to pay a fixed amount of dividend, thus its debt characteristics. On the other hand it can be passed if the company does not perform very well, thus its equity characteristics.

DEBT CAPITAL

These are borrowed funds to finance the business. The borrowed funds are at cost until they are repaid.

Types of Debt capital

Debentures

These are long term loans given to the firm by investors and the terms and conditions contained in the debenture trust deed.

Mortgage bonds

This is a long-term loan which is usually secured over the fixed property of the company and bears a variable interest rate. These are raised over the value of property offered as security.

Loans

This simply involve lending of money by one party to another. Terms and conditions can then be set by the two parties.

Leases

These are sources of finance for funding mostly movable assets. These are secured as the lessor retains ownership of the property, while the lessee uses the property.

The lease payments are computed so as to render the cost of the asset plus a return to the lessor.

LEVERAGES

What is leverage?

It is a relation of your efforts and rewards. According to Dr. T.K. Jain in his article, 'Leverage analysis in financial management', describes it as the one which shows relation between various aspects particularly risk and return.

Types of leverages

1. Operating leverage
2. Financial leverage

Operating leverage

It measures the impact of change in sales volume on Earnings Before Interest and Tax. It measures the riskiness due to fixed cost resources in the organisation.

It is calculated as follows:
Degree of Operating Leverage = $\dfrac{\% \text{ CHANGE IN EBIT}}{\% \text{ CHANGE IN SALES}}$

It measures the impact of fixed cost on profitability.

Financial leverage

This is the use of fixed charge securities like debentures in the overall capital structure

Degree of financial leverage (DFL) tells us about the level of financial risk that we are taking. If financial leverage increases, the risk of the firm increases.

Financial leverage is measured as follows: DFL = $\dfrac{\% \text{ change in net income}}{\% \text{ change in EBIT}}$

DCL= DOL * DFL

This is the product of operating and financial leverages which is called Degree of combined leverage.

Capitalization

This is the decision regarding determining the optimal capital requirement of the business.

COST THEORY - This considers the amount of capitalization on the basis of cost of various assets required to set up and run the business activities.

EARNINGS THEORY - This considers the future expected earnings of the company on the basis of appropriate capitalization rate.

OVER-CAPITALIZATION - This is when there is excess capital than required.

Dangers of over-capitalization

1. Idle and unproductive capital
2. Unnecessary cost of carrying capital
3. Possibility of misuse of capital

Under- capitalization

This is when there is little capital compared to the one required.

The danger is that the business will not be able to purchase some required assets.

Sources of capital

After deciding the capital requirement of the business the main task is to choose the source of finance available so that there is optimal balance between sources.

Sources of capital are as follows:

1. Share capital
2. Debentures
3. Term loans
4. Public Deposits
5. Lease financing
6. Hire purchase
7. Retained earnings

Capital Structure

What is capital structure?

Combination of capital is called capital structure. The firm may use only equity, or only debt, or a combination of equity + debt, or a combination of equity + debt + preference shares or may use other similar combinations.

Carlos Corriea defines capital structure as, "The way in which the financing is arranged"

When one is designing the capital structure he should take into consideration the following;

1. The minimization of the cost of capital
2. The reduction of risk
3. It should be flexible
4. It should give required control to the owners
5. It should enable the firm to have the adequate finance

Risk associated with capital structure is:

1. Business risk
2. Financial risk

Business risk

This is risk relating to the operating activities of the company. It is often reflected by the operating leverage. It is the nature of the industry and the nature of the company's operations. It is also the situation where EBIT may vary due to the in capital structure. It is influenced by the ratio of fixed costs to total costs. If the ratio of fixed costs is higher the business risk is higher.

Financial risk

This is influenced by the balance between equity and debt. It consists of the risk of not being able to cover fixed interest charge (interest risk) and the risk that a liquidation debt has a preferential claim against the assets (capital risk). It is the variability of EPS due to change in capital structure.

EBIT-EPS ANALYSIS

Cost of debt is lower than cost of equity, therefore trading on equity (RAISING DEBT) raises EPS and gives benefit to shareholders. However excess of debt creates more risk, therefore the firm should come up with optimum level of debt and equity.

The Theory of Optimal Capital Structure

The theory states that we can have an optimal capital structure-as we raise the debt we can raise the value of the firm to some extent. Thus level of debt can be raised to a certain level which is the ideal capital structure. The object of the financial manager is to raise wealth and the value of the firm which can be achieved by the ideal capital structure.

Theories of capital structure

Traditional theory

It states that with the use of the debt, the overall cost of capital decreases to some extent there after it increases. This means that the cost of capital with the help of debt decreases to some point the after debt financing becomes detrimental to the company.

Net Income theory

If you raise debt, leverage will increase thereby increasing the overall value of the firm. Debt has lower cost thereby reducing the overall cost of capital.

Value of the firm is calculated as follows;

$V = S + D$

Where V= value of the firm

S= equity

D= debt

An increase in leverage will raise the value of the firm, it increases the EPS. This means it will increase the market price of the shares and reduce the overall weighted cost of capital. This means leverage is always beneficial.

Net operating income approach

This states that capital structure decision is irrelevant. If you raise debt the cost of equity will increase. Therefore the overall cost of capital remains constant in spite of leverage. This states that there is no advantage of raising debt. The market discounts the firm, which is leveraged. Thus capital structure decision is not relevant.

Modigliani-Miller approach

This states that there is no optimal capital structure because irrespective of the level of gearing, a firm's weighted marginal cost of capital will not change. This is because as the company increases its debt (which is cheaper than equity) it is increasing its risk. The equity holders will require compensation for an increase in risk and then the cost of equity will rise and offset the relative benefit of the cheaper debt.

PROFIT MANAGEMENT

This concept dictates all functions and processes within an organisation; and extending to its suppliers and customers, impacts profitability; and continuously needs performance and results. Profit management includes the strategy and decision on how to deliver activities that support the delivery of value to the customer, the cost of channel engagement and product or customer profitability and the assets required to deliver value. This includes cost reduction, working capital improvement and margin improvement.

Companies in emerging and growing markets and industries are forced with the challenge of nurturing the growth and development of their revenue line without eroding their profitability by way of aggressively expanding their cost base.

In emerging environments, most major companies have tried to preserve profitability through head count reduction which by itself has time and again shown paltry correlation to value creation and fail to address the underlying drives of profitability.

The concept of profit management dictates all functions and processes within an organisation and extending from the organisation into its suppliers and customers, impacts profitability and continuously needs measurement and review to optimize performance and results. It includes strategy decision of how to deliver activities that support the delivery of value to the customer, the cost of channel engagement and products or customer profitability and the assets required to deliver value.

Dividend Policy

Dividend - This is a portion of net profits paid by a company to its shareholders. It is usually calculated according to the number of shares each person holds in that particular company. This is called dividend per share (DPS).

Dividend Payment Procedure

The decision to pay a dividend rests within the board of directors. Corporate usually announces the dividend when it presents its results.

Dividend declaration date: The date when the board declares a dividend.

Ex-dividend date: The date on which the people buying the shares are entitled to dividends e.g. all those who bought shares on or before the 4th of June 2010 will be entitled to a dividend. Therefore after this date the share will be trading ex-dividend and cum-dividend before that date.

Payment date: This is the date when the money will be transferred to the respective shareholders.

Forms of dividends

Cash dividend - Shareholders receive their dividends in the form of cash.

Script dividend - the shareholders receive their dividends in the form of company's shares.

Dividend Policy Theories

The residual approach to dividends

This approach contends that dividends are a passive parameter and do not matter in decision-making. They are what is left over after decisions regarding investment and financing have been made. This means that dividends can be paid after the company has invested in all projects that offer a return greater or equal to their required rate of return. To adopt this approach the company must know the following:

- Its set of investment opportunities
- Its required rate of return
- Its target debt ratio

The company must accept all projects exceeding their required rate of return and if there is money left, and then dividends can be paid.

The dividend irrelevance theory

Modigliani and Miller argued that dividends do not affect the wealth of shareholders and as such they do not matter to shareholders, thereby putting forward the following assumptions:

- Perfect markets
- No floatation costs
- A given investment policy

Dividend relevance theory

This is based on the argument of Myron Gordon and John Lintner, which says that investors prefer current dividends and there is a direct relationship between dividend policy and share value. Investors are risk averse and they attach less risk to current dividend than to future dividends or capital growth. This is because investors can then re-invest their dividends. Therefore they would rather receive current dividend, which is certain than receive future dividends, which have an element of uncertainty.

Tax based theories

If the dividend tax is lower than capital gains tax then the firm should pay all its income as a dividend as this reduces the tax paid by the shareholders on their income.

Signal Hypothesis And Clientele Effect

Signal considerations

Observations that have been made on the movement of share prices on stock exchanges after a dividend declaration that:

- When a firm announces an increased dividend the price of shares increases.
- When the firm announces a reduced dividend the prices of the shares decrease
- When the firm's dividends remain constant the price of the shares also remains the same.

Clientele effect

Investors can be placed into different clientele groups. The main clientele groups are those who prefer dividends and those who prefer capital gains.

Investors might prefer dividends because they pay no tax or lower tax on dividend than to capital gains.

Some shareholders prefer dividends because they invest in equity to obtain a regular income.

Other investors prefer capital gains. This clientele group is made up of those who pay no tax or a lower tax rate on capital gains income.

Investors who invest in equity as long-term investment will prefer capital gains as opposed to dividends.

FINANCIAL RATIOS

This is the selection, evaluation, and interpretation of financial data, along with other pertinent information, to assist in investment and financial decision-making.

Classification OF Ratios

A ration is a mathematical relation between one quality and another. Ratios are classified according to the way they are constructed and their general characteristics. The ratios are as follows;

> Coverage ratio - This is a measure of a firm's ability to satisfy particular obligations.
>
> Return ratio - This is a measure of the net benefit, relative to the resources expended.
>
> Turnover ratio - This is a measure of the gross benefit, relative to the resources expended.
>
> Component percentage - This is the ratio of a component of an item to the item.

Ratios give us an indication if we are applying the company's assets efficiently and profitably. These also give us an indication if we are able to meet the financial obligations of the organisation.

Six aspects of operating performance and financial condition we can evaluate from financial ratios.

Liquidity ratio provides information on a firm's ability to meet its short-term obligations.

Profitability ratio provides information on the amount of income from each dollar of sales.

Activity ratio relates information on a firm's ability to manage its resources efficiently.

Return on investment ratio provides information on the amount of profit, relative to the assets employed to produce that profit.

Financial leverage ratio provides information on the degree of a firm's fixed financing obligations and its ability to satisfy these financing obligations.

Shareholder ratio describes the firm's financial condition in terms of amounts per share.

Short-Term solvency

Liquidity reflects the ability of a firm to meet its short-term obligations using assets that are most readily converted into cash. Assets that may be converted into cash in a short period of time are referred to as liquid assets. These are also termed current assets and they are used to satisfy short-term obligations (current liabilities). The amount by which current assets exceeds current liabilities is called net working capital.

Operating cycle

This is the length of time it takes to convert an investment of cash in inventory back into cash.

Number of days inventory – This is the number days inventory on hand can last while it produces cost of sales. This can be calculated as follows:

$$\text{Number of days inventory} = \frac{\text{Inventory}}{\text{Average days' cost of goods sold}}$$

This tells us the no number of days it takes to convert the inventory on hand into cost of sales.

Number of days receivables – This is the number of days it takes to convert accounts receivables into cash.

This can be calculated using the formula below;

$$\text{Number of days receivables} = \frac{\text{accounts receivables}}{\text{Average day's credit}}$$

We can also check how long it takes a firm to pay its short-term obligations. We can apply the same logic as we did to accounts receivables, thus using the formula below:

$$\text{Number of days payables} = \frac{\text{accounts payable}}{\text{Average day's purchases}}$$

Liquidity Ratios

These measure the ability of a firm to generate cash to meet its immediate needs.

Current ratio - This is the ratio of current assets to current liabilities and it indicates the firm's ability to satisfy its current liabilities with its current assets. The formula is as follows:

$$\text{Current ratio} = \frac{\text{current assets}}{\text{Current liabilities}}$$

Quick ratio – This is the ratio of quick assets (current assets less inventory) to current liabilities and it indicates the firm's ability to satisfy current liabilities with its most liquid assets. The formula is as follows:

$$\text{Quick ratio} = \frac{\text{current assets - inventory}}{\text{Current liabilities}}$$

Profitability and Activity ratios

Profitability ratios - These compare components of income with sales.

Gross profit margin - This is the gross profit to sales ratio and it indicates how much of every dollar of sales is left after cost of sales.

It is calculated as follows:

$$\text{Gross profit margin} = \frac{\text{Sales - cost of sales}}{\text{Sales}}$$

Operating profit margin – This is the operating income (EBIT) to sales ratio and it indicates how much of each dollar of sales is left over operating expenses.

It is calculated as follows:

$$\text{Operating profit margin} = \frac{\text{EBIT}}{\text{Sales}}$$

Net profit margin – This is the ratio of net income to sales and it indicates how much of each dollar of sales is left over after all expenses.

It is calculated as follows:

$$\text{Net profit margin} = \frac{\text{Net income}}{\text{Sales}}$$

FUNDS FLOW AND CASHFLOW STATEMENTS

Cash flow Statements

This is a summary of the firm's cash flows, summarized by operations, investment activities, and financing activities. It reports a company's change in cash and cash equivalents from one balance sheet date to another. It classifies the amount of change according to operating, investment and financing activities.

<u>Cash flow from operating activities</u> - This is cash flow from day to day operations. It is usually adjusted with non-cash items, changes in working capital accounts.

<u>Cash flow from investment activities</u> - These are cash flows related to the acquisition of fixed assets and proceeds from the sale of the same assets.

<u>Cash flow from financing activities</u> - These are cash flows from activities related to the sources of capital funds e.g. pay dividends and issue bonds.

Purpose of Cash flow statements

Cash flow statements are intended to disclose information that is not available from the mere inspection of the financial statements (income statement and balance sheet). Cash flow statements indicate how cash was generated and used and this is necessary as cash is the lifeline of organisations. Cash flow statement provides information about a company's gross receipts and gross payments for a specified time. It reports changes in cash and cash equivalents between two balance sheet dates.

Uses of cash flow statements

Cash flow statements are used to review past events and assess the future cash flows. Cash flows also show the relationship between profitability and cash generation ability.

Funds Flow Statements

This reports the change in working capital from one balance sheet date to another.

BUDGETS AND BUDGETORY CONTROL SYSTEMS

What is a budget?

It is a quantitative expression of a plan of action prepared in advance of the period to which it relates; this is according to T. Lucey in his book, 'Costing third edition of 1992'.

Budgets can be prepared for the business or the whole organisation or for certain sections e.g. sales budget.

In brief the preparation of the budget means translation of the objectives of the organisation into detailed feasible action plan.

Budgetary control

This is the aspect of checking actual perfomance against the budget and reporting on variances. This will help to keep expenditure within agreed limits. Deviations are noted and corrective action is taken.

Benefits of budgeting

Planning and coordination

The process of budgeting works within the framework of long term and the overall objectives to produce operational plans for the organisations. Planning is the key success to every organisation and budgeting forces planning to take place.

Clarification of authority and responsibility

The process of budgeting clarifies the responsibility of each section or department. The adoption of budgets authorises the plans contained in it and this enables management by exception to be practised.

Communication

The budgetary process involves all levels of management. Budget is therefore an important tool of communication at management levels regarding the organisational objectives and the practical problems of implementing these problems. Budgets require communication within departments so as to coordinate the action plans as outlined by the budget.

Motivation

The involvement of lower and middle management staff in the establishment of targets of which performance can be judged, has been a motivator to lower levels.

The budgetary period

Budgeting must be related to a specific period of time ranging from long term to short term. These can be broken into shorter monthly periods for implementation and easy budgetary control and monitoring. Because of the changing conditions in the economy budgets are reviewed periodically.

Limiting factor or principal budget factor

A limiting factor is those factors, which at any given time, will effectively limits the activities of the organisation. Because such constraint will have an effect on all plans and budgets it will have to be identified during the budgeting process and its effect considered carefully.

Fixed and Flexible budgets

Fixed budget - This is defined as budget which is designated to remain unchanged irrespective of volume or output attained. It is a budget with no analysis of costs.

Flexible budget - This is a budget which is designated to adjust the permitted cost levels to suit the levels of activity attained.

The fixed budget is necessary at the planning stage when it serves to define the objectives of the organisation. It is of less value thereafter for control purposes except if the level of budgeted activity is actually attained.

Human aspects of budgeting

The human subjective aspects in budgeting can be classified as below:

Goal congruence

This means that the goals of individuals and groups should coincide with the goals and objectives of the organisation. There should be recognition that the organisation objectives cannot be imposed through the budgeting process without considering the influences of a certain group or departmental objectives. There is evidence that authority imposed from above is less effective than authority accepted from below. Goal congruence is enhanced when there is a more participative management style than the emphasis on hierarchy and authority.

Participation

Budgets can either be imposed by top management or be crafted by means of participation of the budget holders. Participation will increase the understanding of the organisational objectives and makes organisational goals to be understood by all the individuals concerned. If people participate in the budget process they will feel more part of the team and be highly motivated.

Goal definition

People work more efficiently when they have clearly defined targets and objectives. This means that personal goals should coincide with organisational goals. Clearly defined goals, agreed and accepted by the individuals concerned will encourage goal congruence and increase motivation.

Types of budgets

Cash budget

This is a summary that shows the expected cash receipts and cash payments during the budget period.

Production budget

This is the budget, which shows forecasted production for the period.

Sales budget

This is the budget, which shows forecasted sales for the budget period.

Master budget

This is the overall forecast of the organisational expectations for the budget period and is the combination of all types of budgets.

CORPORATE RESTRUCTURING

Companies restructure so as to change their financial strategy or to help correct a market under-pricing. These changes in financial strategy normally relate to a reduction in gearing. This can be done through selling assets or raising new funds. It also takes negotiations with creditors and swapping debt into equity.

Where the company has a wrong financial strategy, the strategy might be wrong because the company has too little debt and remains financed by equity. The company will then need to re-balance its debt / equity ratio. The company can correct this by paying out a special dividend or undertake a share buyback. The company can also use the investor's money by investing in a value enhancing investment opportunity.

Fall in operating profits may lead to problems for a company, which has too much gearing, and these problems are mainly debt problem strategies. These can be solved as follows;

- Raise cash by selling assets, either outright sell of surplus or in a sale-and-leaseback transaction.

- Raise cash by issuing new equity or another financial instrument.

- Arrange with creditors to restructure existing debt.

Selling Assets

If the company has surplus assets it can sale to raise cash. These assets should not be necessary for operations. The issues, which can arise with the sale of assets, are:

- Determining which assets are core.

- Finding a buyer

- Being prepared to take accounting consequences (loss on disposal)

Raising new finance

In order to come out of the financial problems the company needs to raise new finance from existing or new investors. This may be through raising equity from existing shareholders including a deep discount right issue. The company can also raise funds in the form of convertible.

Re-negotiating debt

Re-structuring debt is also another way of reconstruction. To aid the company's short-term survival the company can swap debt into equity to its leaders. In this case existing loans will be released. The impact of finance costs can be eliminated. The argument is that if the creditors insist on their debt being serviced the company might go into liquidation and they will lose their money.

Re-organisations to address market perceptions

When the problem is not internally, but relates to the fact that the company is trading at market value considerable below a fair value for its shares. The solutions will be as follows;

- Demerger, to demonstrate the value in the group
- Blitz on public relations to change market perceptions
- Take the company private

Demerger- this is a transaction which one listed company become two or more listed companies, generally with the same shareholders. This is different from an equity carve out where the subsidiary company (or generally only a minority stake) is sold to the public as an initial public offering.

The transaction will not be termed a reconstruction unless the business disposed of or formed a substantial percentage of the overall group value.

Why demerger?

It is undertaken to improve the value attributed to the business by the financial markets. When a group consists of two or more different classes of business, it might make it difficult for analysts and shareholders to understand and such lack of understanding may lead to under-pricing in the markets.

After a demerger each separate company can then make its financial decisions according to its operations.

Restructuring takes place when a company is in financial trouble or is undervalued by the financial markets. The company's restructuring plans may of necessity change as market conditions become more or less favourable.

INTERNATIONAL BUSINESS FINANCE

International financial management enables firms to operate in markets much larger than those provided by the domestic economy. International business finance is still concerned with maximising the shareholder value but with new risk involved. International business finance is therefore concerned with managing the additional risk associated with the firm's choice to operate internationally.

International structure of organisations

International structure or operation arises due to the following:

- When a company produces products in one country but sells some or all the products in another country.

- When a company produces products in one country but imports some or all of its raw materials from another country.

- When a company establishes a branch in another country.

- When a company makes international investments.

- When a company establishes international business relationships e.g. patents, franchises or any of such agreements.

WHY FIRMS INVEST INTERNATIONALLY

- To diversify risk

- To extend the market base of the firm

- To provide services to the foreign market

- To take advantage of good investment opportunities

Forms of risk arising from international operations

TRANSACTION RISK

This refers to the exposure to financial risk arising out of individual transactions. This risk arises where one party has a foreign commitment. This is due to the fact that the paying company may end up paying more in local currency due to depreciation of the local currency. Transaction risk usually affects the Profit and Loss of the company.

COMMERCIAL RISK

This refers to the risk of the loss or gain of a market due to changes in currency exchange rates.

POLITICAL RISK

This risk arises from the actions or inactions of governments e.g. imposition or removal of exchange controls, imposition or removal of taxes, imposition or removal of trade tariffs and quotas.

The Foreign Exchange Market

This market offers three facilities as follows:

- Spot exchanges which refer to an immediate purchase or sale of one currency in terms of another at a spot rate.
- Forward exchange which is an agreement to buy or sell now, foreign exchange for delivery at a specified time in the future.
- Swap contract.

DETERMINANTS OF EXCHANGE RATES

a. Interest rate parity - differential interest rates will cause funds to move from a country with lower interest rates to a country with higher interest rates and according to the interest rate parity theory for equilibrium to be reached. Interest rate parity theory explains the difference between the spot and the forward exchange rate by stating that the interest differential between countries is the only determinant of the difference in exchange rates.

b. Purchasing power parity - This theory considers the relationship of exchange rates between two trading countries and states that comparable goods should sell at equivalent values when translated into a second currency (the law of one price).

c. Balance of payments - The exchange rate is greatly influenced by the balance of payments position of a country. A balance of payment surplus causes currency of a country to appreciate whilst the balance of payment deficit causes the currency to depreciate.

CREDIT RATING

This is the estimation of the credit worthiness of an individual, corporation or even a country. It is the evaluation of potential borrower's ability to repay the debt, prepared by a credit bureau at the request of the lender; this is according to Black's Law dictionary.

Credit ratings are calculated from financial history and current assets and liabilities.

Credit Score - This is a statistical method to determine the likelihood of an individual paying back the money he or she has borrowed.

What makes up a credit score?

When you borrow money, your lender sends information to a credit bureau which details, in the form of credit report, how well you handled your debt. From the information in the credit report, the bureau determines a credit score based on five major factors as follows;

   a) Previous credit performance

   b) Current level of indebtedness

   c) Time credit has been in use

   d) Types of credit available

   e) Pursuit of new credit

Although all these factors are included in credit score calculations, they are not given equal weighting.

The weights can be as below:

Previous credit performance	40%
Current level of indebtedness	25%
Time credit has been in use	15%

Types of credit available	15%
Pursuit of new credit	5%

Credit rating is mostly affected by your historical propensity for paying off your debt, therefore your credit rating can be boosted by you having been paying your debts faster. You also need to maintain low levels of indebtedness.

Why your credit rating is important?

When you try to borrow or get services in credit your credit rating is checked. Credit reporting makes it easier for organisation to accept your debit cards and cheques.

Depending on credit score, lenders will determine what risk you pose to them. According to financial theory, increased credit risk means that risk premium must be added to the price at which money is borrowed. If you have a poor credit score lenders will not shun you (unless if it is awful) instead they will lend you at a higher rate than the one paid by someone with a better credit score.

ASSETS AND LIABILITIES MANAGEMENT

This is a risk management technique, which companies employ in managing the assets and liabilities so that an adequate return may be earned. It is also known as surplus management.

By managing a company's assets and liabilities you are able to influence net earnings, which may translate into increased prices.

It can also be defined as matching an individual's assets, for example; if someone is planning to buy a car you decide whether to pay cash, thus lowering assets or to take out a loan thereby increasing debts. Such decisions should be based on interest rates, earning power and on the comfort level with debt.

Financial institutions carry out assets and liabilities management when they match the maturity of their deposits with the length of their loan commitments to keep from being adversely affected by rapid changes in interest rates.

Active management of a bank's balance sheet to maintain a mix of loans and deposits consistent with its goals for long-term growth and risk management is part of assets and liabilities management in banking institutions.

Banks assume financial risk by making loans at interest rates that differ from rates paid in deposits. Deposits usually have shorter maturities than loans and adjust to current market rates faster than loans. The result is a balance sheet mismatch between assets and liabilities.

The function of assets and liabilities management is to measure and control three levels of financial risk as below

1. Credit risk - The probability of default

2. Interest rate risk - The pricing difference between loans and deposits.

3. Liquidity risk - Occurring when loans and deposits have different maturities. This is when there is insufficient liquid assets to meet the liabilities.

The function of assets and liabilities management is managing Net Interest Margin (NIM), that is, the net difference between interest earning assets (loans) and interest paying assets (deposits) to produce consistent growth in the loan portfolio and shareholder earnings.

Gap Analysis

One way to measure the direction and extent of asset-liability mismatch is by using the gap analysis. This is the difference between the amounts of rate sensitive assets (RSA) and rate sensitive liabilities (RSL).

Management of liquidity risk

- There is need to make sure that funds are available as and when liabilities are due.
- Liquidity through maturity and cash flow matching
- Maturity ladder and circulation of cumulative surplus or deficits at selected dates.

Management of interest rate risk

- Impact on Net Interest Income
- Long-term impact on market value or net worth techniques
- Gap analysis
- Duration gap analysis
- Simulation
- Value risk

Conclusion

Assets and liabilities management is the decision making process for controlling risk of existence, stability and growth of a system through dynamic balances of its assets and liabilities.

It is also a technique designed to earn an adequate return while maintaining a comfortable surplus of assets beyond liabilities. It takes into consideration interest rates, earning power and degree of willingness to take a debt.

BIBLIOGRAPHY

Investment management by G. Muponda, 2004

Costing by T. LUCEY, 3RD EDITION, 1989

Financial management by Carlos Correia, 2nd impression, 1995

Global corporate finance by Sukkim and Seng H. Kim, 6th edition, 2006

Fundamental Aspects of Financial Management by Steyn, Warren and Jonker, 1998

Leverage analysis in financial management by Dr.T.K. Jain 2009

The Global Financial System Project by Havard business School

www.ingramcontent.com/pod-product-compliance
Lightning Source LLC
Chambersburg PA
CBHW030035230526
45472CB00002B/526